POSTLUDE

POSTLUDE

A COLLECTION OF POEMS

RUSS PEERY

authorHOUSE®

AuthorHouse™
1663 Liberty Drive
Bloomington, IN 47403
www.authorhouse.com
Phone: 1-800-839-8640

Published by AuthorHouse   08/29/2012

ISBN: 978-1-4772-6246-7 (sc)
ISBN: 978-1-4772-6297-9 (e)

Library of Congress Control Number: 2012915185

This book is printed on acid-free paper.

POSTLUDE

CONTENTS

FOREWORD

My therapist wife says, "People don't do something over and over again unless they get something out of it." That is why I write poems. I get a lot out of it. First is the satisfaction of creativity—being involved in making something, hopefully worthwhile. Second is the pleasure of sharing. That may involve a little presumption, but a little of it is OK. And last is anticipating various responses. If there were no feedback, I would have ceased writing. When I began to get serious about my poetry, expectations included the hope for responses.

Over the years I've put together a few booklets of my writings. The last one, I considered to be my last. After all, I am getting heavy with years. I did not anticipate meeting a woman a couple of decades younger than I with vast amounts of energy and computer savvy, who was excited about what I write. She, Joanne Schwandes, has been the catalyst for this final endeavor, which, I must admit, may not be my final endeavor. Not only is she a great enabler, but she's adding her photographic skills to make this more than just a collection of my poetry. In a real way, together we offer you the following pages.

Russ Peery
28 July 2012
Kissimmee FL

RELATIONSHIPS

STILL WELL ENOUGH TO CHOOSE

While she sleeps
an early morning sleep
I write.

At night
when I begin my sleep
she reads.

There are these hours
when we go our separate ways
silently agreed upon.

And yet we can't remember when
the pattern first emerged
to shape these days of being old
while we're still well enough to choose.

HAPPENSTANCE

If there had not been
a tragic accident in '68
and if a friend had not
told her about the job in '71
we would have never met.
And I would not have
opened my office door
to meet her had I been
a happily married man.
Conventional wisdom
suggested our demise
as did our early days
together, but somehow
we survived long enough
to have grown old together
and have found more love
than anyone could have
suspected. We do not want
to deal with the contingencies
that time will eventually invoke
and sometimes it seems
we are holding our breath.

OUR DIFFERENT TEMPOS PLAY

I wait for her in the morning—
I the early riser.

I leave her reading in the evening
and turn toward dreams
before her sleeping time.

Many hours are there beneath our roof
when we're not together.
It wasn't always this way
and I'm uncertain when it all began.

But it is a good life here in this house
where our different tempos play—
more love now
than when our passions reigned.

LOVE LETTERS

Every week or so
I find upon my bed
next to my dresser
little stacks of folded clothes
that have been washed and dried.
The one who shares the years with me
calls those little stacks "Love Letters."

Every now and then
I'll write a special poem for her.
That's my way of caring.

I'm not much good at laundry.

WATCHING (AN ANNIVERSARY POEM)

Sometimes when you are reading
and I watch you
you are unaware.
Sometimes when you are busy in the kitchen
and I watch you
you are unaware
Sometimes you are folding clothes—
and you are unaware.
I care so much just watching.

Sometimes I wish I'd known you
when you were two.
I would have watched you grow
seeing all those many stages we go through
until the decades call us to be old.
But I only intercepted you
when you were half the age
you've now become.
Though I've been denied my wish
I've not been one deprived.

SHE PUT FRESH FLOWERS

She put fresh flowers in the vase.
Every day
she put fresh flowers in the vase
as I was wilting.

I think she wished
those flowers would breathe—
would breathe into my soul.

And sure enough
I felt them stir—
I felt their breath as hope—
hope requiring
my short supply of patience
to endure.

She put fresh flowers in the vase.
I think
she'll come again tomorrow.

TO CARE FOR AND TO CHERISH

To be cared for
is not the same as
to be cherished
and he was cared for
but not cherished
when he was a little one.

He did not discern this
until recently
when in conversation
it dawned on him
that that was how it was
way back before he can remember.

I think that he has learned to cherish
but it's been
a long, long time in coming.

CHILD CARE

I followed a toddler—
a little girl with curls
who was intrigued
with the sidewalks
we have here.
I kept her safe
and from wandering
too far.
I wondered as I watched
how the baby Jesus was
when a similar age.
There were those
who kept him safe
for a little while
but, in time
he got away—
went his own way—
and those who
cared for him
could not stop
the danger though
they saw it coming.

CHRISTMAS PAGEANTS

I sat next to a mother.
There were many mothers there—
a few fathers—
a smattering of grandparents
of whom I was the oldest.
Most of the mothers had cameras—
the cell phone kind
and more sophisticated ones.
When Joseph and Mary appeared
some mothers' arms flew up
from around the audience
and the cameras went to work.
When the shepherds came
more photographic work ensued.
When the wise men appeared
even more lifted arms were extended.
It was annoying
to this 20th century man
but that's how it is now
when tiny children welcome Jesus
and make parents and grands so proud.
I went to two pageants in two days.
Jesus would be proud of me.

GOOD GRIEF

In canine heaven the dogs are climbing trees
and all the cats, their refuge is denied.
Bones are scattered all around the ground
and scents are better than the ones on earth.
There are no tails that do not wag a bit
and watering all things vertical is allowed.
Barking is encouraged by the angels.

So when you bid farewell to him or her
just take a trip with your imagination
and find pleasure in the possibilities.

LIMITS

When you hear bad news
and it's not YOUR bad news
you may become pensive for a while—
you may suspend some laughter.
But you will sleep as usual
and awaken to begin another day
quite possibly forgetting
the tragic information you received
just yesterday.
And when it surfaces once more
if it surfaces at all
it will have traveled some
from your parameters.

This does not mean that you're indifferent—
but there are limits to your caring.
And, admit it:
there are likely many others
whose capacities for empathy
exceed your own.

SOMEONES

There is the feeling you feel
when your see something
so compelling
that you wish someone
was there with you
to share it.

And the someone
may become someones
and they may be
near or far away.

They may be gone—
perhaps long gone.
When I had my first coffee
this morning
the sunrise demanded
that I watch it.
So I sat right down
in a chair facing east.

As I absorbed
the beauty of the sky
I thought of someone
and then of someones
and then more someones—
and quite possibly
I thought of you.

THE FEEL OF A HOUSE

The feel of a house
changes
when one who helps fill it
goes away
and becomes expected.
You create the same effect
when you leave
and become the expected one.
The rooms
may seem to stay the same
but the art on the walls
and the furniture in the various rooms
will be experienced
in a different way
when a certain one's presence
is absent.
Whatever it is
it comes to the house
in silence
and leaves unnoticed
when the expected one
returns.

THE ITCH

The writer of Proverbs
may have had a problem
similar to one that I have sometimes.

Long ago, divinely inspired, he wrote:
"Two is better than one."

The problem is
when I have an itch
in certain places on my back
that I cannot reach.

Back scratchers just don't cut it.
Leaning against a wall and wiggling
helps a little.

The best solution
is finding another to stand behind you
and you verbally guide that person
until the exact location of the itch is found
and then he or she commences scratching.

"Two is better than one."

THE LATEST ADDITION

The little guy and I
were eye to eye
when I sat on the floor.
To him I was a curiosity—
to me he was a possibility:
a man in the making—
possibly living 'til the century's end.
He was not yet walking
nor was he talking
but was getting ready to do both.
I watched him move about
and then look back at me and smile.
I'll take him with me in my prayers tonight
and he'll forget me
when I leave his sight.

THE LITTLE NURSE

The little nurse
not much taller than the cart she pushed
up and down the corridors
stopped frequently—
read charts and opened drawers
containing a variety of pills.
She then dispensed the designated medications
and patients' needs were tended to.

When she first conceived that she might be a nurse
could she have fathomed
her life would be like this?

I wondered when she came to me
with countenance so pleasing
and handed me a cup of water—
but I never asked her.

I no longer need her ministrations
but seem to have a need to think of her:
the little nurse
not much taller than the cart she pushed.

THE SMILE

I never saw her not smiling.
Wheeled into the nursing home dining room
she always leaned slightly to the right.
It was her smile that got my attention—
on a mouth through which no words passed.
When fed slowly it enlarged slightly.

I wondered how and when that smile began—
what struck her down to make it permanent.
Surely there was a time
when there was animation on her lips.

I thought about her very first smile as an infant—
her laughter as a little girl—
smiles she must have shared with her loved ones.

Those who care for her now, month after month
are probably used to that smile—
don't pay it much attention.
But I did, day after day, until I was discharged.
Though I've forgotten most everyone else there
I can't seem to forget her.

THE TAP ON THE SHOULDER

I can still feel
(though it was years ago)
the tap on my left shoulder
as I sat in symphony hall
in Nashville
made by the woman
sitting behind me
as the intermission began.
She leaned over and said:
"You have beautiful hair."

I met a man the other day
with similar hair.
We talked about it
and concluded that
that was the best thing
we had going for us—
that from the top of our heads
downward
we had less and less
to be pleased about.

THOSE "ONCE UPON A TIMES"

She kept the diamond ring
though at the time
she said she'd send it back.
I guess I owed her that—
I, the one who changed his mind.
Thirty years then passed
and I saw her once again.
She had survived.
She even thrived.

This morning
as I read a WHAT IF poem
I was reminded once again of that event—
now sixty years ago.

I think that as we age
and reach that stage
of short-term memory loss
we are apt to often call up
our "Once Upon A Times".

TO BE A MEMORY

She hopes to be a memory
for her grandchildren.
There's always the possibility
that they'll look back
and not recall her.

So when does it begin?
How old must they be
which leads to
how old will she be?

Of course
she'd like to be with them forever—
at least through high school.
And how about the wedding
and maybe great-grandchildren?

She's greedy
for more years than she can count.

VERBOSITY

When words flow like a waterfall
pouring from an unfamiliar mouth
(almost a stranger)
and you're beneath the flow
with hardly any place to go
you sneak a look at your watch
hoping that your furtive overture
will somehow make the flowing cease
and bring relief.
You're quite polite and do not turn away
until the speaker has his say.

But you will later tell a friend
who listens as you tell about the waterfall
and he will let you know when you've become one.

TRANSITIONS

A HOUSE DEMOLISHED

Driving by that house I went to town.
When I returned I saw they'd torn it down.
Long empty, still beautiful, but in disrepair
I was shocked to see it wasn't there.
In its place a pile of wood and stone
where once it stood
and it was someone's home.
Folks dwelled there and they talked and slept.
They laughed and hoped and joked
and no doubt wept.

Someday I know the house I live in now
will share a similar fate—will fall somehow.
Will there be some stranger passing by
who will see its rubble and will sigh?
It is likely I will never see
what will be this small catastrophe.
By then I'll likely be in heaven or hell
or in a place where all dead poets dwell.

BETTER DAYS?

Oh my, oh me,
"the best is yet to be"
has come and gone
and Browning's song
eventually is wrong.
How do we cope
with little hope
that life will offer better days
than what has been?
And if we've left no legacy
that's worth a pot of gold
our growing old
requires that we be bold
and tough as nails.
I made myself that tough
but I don't wield the hammer.
And if it's God that does
I pray He doesn't bend me
but hits me straight
until I'm fastened well
to history.

ENDANGERED STRANGERS

When my computer
becomes obsolete
it is likely
to end up in China
in some waste dump
near some rural town
where its toxic insides
will be ripped apart
by some poor strangers
endangered
because of economic realities
that force them
to deal with
what the world doesn't want
and doesn't have good plans
to get rid of.

GOD'S FINGER

The old woman
while driving
misjudged
and was nearly
demolished
by a car whose driver
managed
to swerve
and miss her.

As the young man
went on his way
he gave her "The Finger."

She viewed this as
 "God's finger"
pointing at her and
suggesting
that it was time
for her
to give up driving.

She did drive home
but laid her keys
on the kitchen table
and has not driven since.

She is most grateful
that The Lord Almighty
used
the wrath of a young man
to set her straight.

HOUSED IN A TORTOISE SHELL

There was a time back long ago
I thought the world I'd change.
That time has passed and it didn't last
and the world stays much the same.

The world changed me more than I changed it
as my destiny unraveled.
Now I've grown old—am far less bold
than in the days I traveled.

All around me I see my zealous peers
quite seriously involved.
They do whatever they can do—
as much as years allow.

But I'm now housed in a tortoise shell
and seldom venture forth.
Some folks may think I've gone to hell.
I disagree, of course.

THE CORRIDOR OF TIME

The corridor of time
that I've walked through
for many years
has slowly narrowed—
almost imperceptibly—
almost.
But I've noticed lately
there's less room to maneuver.

EVERY DAY BEGUILES

When young I didn't know about the years—
that they speed by faster than expected.
My agenda left some things neglected
that later on I thought about with tears.

Middle age did little to prepare me
to deal well with time's amazing speed.
Passing calendars, I paid little heed
to when they changed, though it was plain to see.

Now I'm aware that I am fairly old
and hardly recognize the world I knew
when youth consumed me. I am nearly through
yet not disheartened to see the years unfold.

I have been around a little while
and still I find that every day beguiles.

I STILL CHASE RHYMES

I've watched the decades come and go.
As I grow old there's less I know.
There was a time I was involved—
took interest in and problem solved
the things I thought that needed me.
But now there's much that I can see
that I might possibly deplore
but find it easy to ignore.
I'm satisfied to sit and stare
at things that once demanded care
from me. My garden's full of weeds
and I pull not, though I see needs.
I still may try to write a little
but my prowess I'll belittle.
I can't deny that I've declined
but, I find, I still chase rhymes.

MEDITATION FOILED

There was no wind
and all the leaves were still.
Tall grasses held no motion
and all the birds were mute.

I was embraced by solitude
and found my meditation easy to maintain.
I'd found an inner peace.

But then a fly flew by
and buzzed around my ear
and vanished.
My meditation ceased.
Serenity dissolved
and all the noble thoughts I had
flew from my head—
to join the fly perhaps.

POSTLUDE

My postlude
has commenced
I must admit—
no doubt about it.

It need not be brief.
I hope its proper length
will be achieved.

My postlude
is played out
in my quotidian dailyness.

It will unfold
with many things
I can't control.

But I'll have room
for choosing.

THE LOST WORD

I had a word and lost it—
on the tip of my tongue
and it dissolved.
Or did I drop it somewhere
I can't find it.
It must be there somewhere
just beyond my reach.

I get angry at this lostness
and embarrassed, too
when I'm speaking to someone.
My discomfort is noticed
and I'm told
"Don't worry about it"—
or "It will come to you."
Sometimes the lost word gets found
and sometimes it doesn't.

I wish I'd harvested more words
when acquisition was easy.
If I had a lot more
maybe I'd miss the one lost, less.
But I'll never really know about that.

What I do know is that I mourn just a tad
when I reach down into my word well
and come up with something
that does not quench my thirst.

SOLUTIONS

I was cold
and able to find warmth—
was too warm
and able to find coolness—
was hungry
and able to find food—
was hurt
and was able to find healing.
I became old
and still am old—
still looking for solutions.

RHYTHM

In his latter years
when he was in decline
he read the New York Times
while sitting at a table.
When he wasn't reading
he stared out of the window
taking in the waters of the Sound.
There was a rhythm to his days
broken by another rhythm:
dialysis three times a week
for several years.
As he grew less able by his table
the Times was less devoured.
At last it came to pass
that the front page
was all the he could scan.
And now his chair is empty—
the Times lies on the table
and waves still come upon the shore—
their rhythm undiminished.

THE ICE CUBES

The drink is gone, but not the ice cubes.

Shrunk some since they began to cool my tea
they nestle in the bottom of the glass
and slowly melt.
They seem translucent silver
as they reflect the lamp light
filling up this room where I recline and write.
Their shapes, once cubicle are now quite varied
and keep on changing.
And as they do, a residue of water
forms beneath them.
Occasionally I take a sip.
The flavor of the tea is gone.
I will watch a little longer
as they liquefy before my eyes.
I'll leave for slumber pretty soon
and as I sleep they'll disappear.
And when I see the glass tomorrow
I'll see only vestiges
of what I write about tonight.

THE NURSING HOME

They've fallen in the battlefields of life.
Some heroes there, some undistinguished—
their final homes in little rooms with beds.
And there are people there
more mentally alert than I
and others who have lost their way
within the jungles of their minds.

People, out of duty—out of love
come by to hold their hands—
sometimes to share some history—
or some gossip or a joke—
sometimes just to sit in silence.

No one foretold how this would be—
these final chapters of those lives
that once held promises—
some realized and some not kept.

We who live outside those walls
that harbor those who need more care than we
may never join our peers within—
but then again, we might.

THE ROAD YOU'LL TRAVEL

You've no choice but to take it
for its name is TOMORROW
and it offers hopes and fears
and joys or sorrows
and laughter and tears
or just some ordinary days
depending on your luck
or your karma
or whatever it is
that leads you on
through this life
and the next—
if there is a next.
You can't see far ahead
because of the curves
and maybe that's just as well.
It's hard to tell.

THE VELOCITY OF DARKNESS

I go up and down nursing home corridors
behind my walker wearing my black tee shirt
which has a white question imposed on it
that covers my chest:
WHAT IS THE SPEED OF DARK?

Folks confronted by this tall man
take furtive glances
and think I might be slightly crazy—
give me quick nods, then move on.

I am soliciting entertainment
which only I appreciate.
This helps me get through my day—
this pretense of measuring
the velocity of darkness.

I've seen enough here to think
I know a little bit about it.

THE WINDOW SHADES

The window shades are drawn at night.
To peeping toms I'd be a sight
if shades stayed up and showed me off—
a man of more than eighty years
the best of which has disappeared.

The window shades are raised at dawn
providing that there's nothing wrong
with my body's resurrection.
I never see one looking in
to gaze upon my aging skin.

WORDS FOR THE EYES

He hears the sounds of words
but often
not enough for understanding—
as if a foreign tongue is spoken.
That's how it is with him.
Even when he strains
deciphering defies his efforts
to assemble meaning.
Thus he withdraws from mingling
savoring the world
where words are for the eyes.

THEIR YIELDING TIME

The OLD can't say they've been deprived of years—
cannot complain they've not been given time
to do some good in life. And as they near
its end sometimes they feel they stand in line
to step upon that threshold none can see
across. Perhaps they're into counting blessings
or maybe weighing losses. They hope to be
remembered some beyond their final resting.

They write the final chapter of their lives
amazed they've come so soon. And some of them
are ready to pass on while others thrive
and wish to stay to see what still might happen.
This is their yielding time. It's come so fast.
Their suns are low. Will they be free at last?

REFLECTION

A MERRY CHASE

I am bothered by my mind some days
because it does not travel
where I think it ought to go
or where I wish it to.
My thoughts seem out of my control
and yet I follow them around.
They lead my on a merry chase
and I have little choice
but to pursue.
My brain's meandering
moves up and down the landscape of my mind:
ridiculous to the sublime—
boring to fascinating—
depressing to hilarious—
flighty to focused—
sometimes a bit embarrassing.

I wonder
if there are other folks
that God has made this way.

CONVERSATION CATALYST

Sometimes
there's a lull in the conversation
and he waits
thinking someone will fill the void.
If, after a long pause
no one does
he feels obligated
to keep things going.
His discomfort level rises
when silence is prolonged.
He assumes
"anything is better than nothing".
He knows some jokes—some gossip.
He is good at "the weather".
He avoids politics.
He is like oil lubricating sluggish dialog.
He is an enabler—a catalyst.
But no one knows
what he really thinks.

DEPRIVED OF MYSTERY

If I had expected life
to turn out as it has
I wonder if I'd be better off
for all the knowing.

Deprived of mystery
fate's unfolding
could be boring.
Or we might wince
at what we know will come to pass.

To know the score
before the game starts
isn't what makes
our worlds go round.

I USED TO THINK

I used to think
that youthful zeal
gave way to wisdom.

It seemed to me
God would employ
that methodology.

But God did not!

Sometimes
it works that way.

But
our neighbor has dementia
and his wife became our friend.

We talk about the end
and we're dismayed.

LEGACY

Tomorrow
I will ship
three dozen rattles
to a shop in Asheville.
I, through my production,
have entertained
in thirty swiftly passing years
at least twelve thousand babies.

Held first in my hands
to fashion and to shape
later
tiny fingers grasp them—
then the rattles rattle.
They've rattled in the USA
and far across the sea.

This, my legacy—
this, a portion of my history
should be in my obituary.

MY MIND AND WALKING

I have concluded
after a bit of concluding
that my mind
tends to wander into various places—
but especially into three places
as I take my walks in the morning.

The first to dominate
are the things that I'm reading.
They're apt to consume my mind
as I step along—sometimes.
Lately, I've been dealing with
the Titanic and Auschwitz
in my ventures with my Kindle.
I am appalled and mystified
by the noble and the gruesome
as knowledge seeps into my ignorance.

Or I may play with the dynamics of
folks I know, both young and old,
as I stride along my morning route.
From concern about jerks and saints
and many in between.

I'm provided with material
that swims around my head.

There is so much pleasure—
some disappointment.

Then there're those days when
I pay serious attention
to the beauty that surrounds me—
the songs of the birds, the swaying of trees—
the ripples on water, the feel of the wind.

I can't predict how my head will deal
with the possibilities that surround me
and only when I get home and reflect
do I grasp where I have traveled
on that same old walk I take in the mornings.

MEATLOAF SANDWICH

When
she saved the spider
from a drain death
and carefully placed it
on a Kleenex
and delivered it
beyond the open window
to some kind of freedom
she did not think
of her noonday meal—
a meatloaf sandwich:
courtesy of cattle.

MEDITATION

The sun was low
my shadow long
and the shadows of the trees
longer and wider than mine.
I strolled along beside those trees
and in and out of shadows.
As I walked my shadow disappeared
and then soon reappeared.
Had it changed in that brief moment
when it vanished and then came back?
Or was it the same
when it came out on the other side?

When I meditate I feel as if
I briefly disappear—
get lost in something larger than I.
And when I return am I the same
or have I changed?

THE KITE POEM

The kite was a poem
I launched into the sky
and I held it with a string of ink.
The kite danced to cadences
stirred by the wind—
and it looked beautiful up there—
so beautiful I wished to pull it down
and share with you.
But the string broke
and the poem fluttered and fell down
and though I searched
I could not find it.

THE SEND OFF

Most dawns come so slowly
that you don't really see the light's increase—
it's just that you're aware it's getting brighter.

Most days are born that way—gradually.
I find in their gradual coming
a great time for pondering
how it is
and how it was
and how it will be
as the day unfolds.

Yesterday I ventured to think
how it used to be
when my mother sent me off to school.

THE THINKER

Rodin's "The Thinker"
hadn't greeted me
for more than thirty years.
Yesterday, in Nashville
we met again
and once again I studied him
and noted I had changed
since last we met in Philadelphia—
that he had stayed the same.

While standing by The Thinker, thinking
I thought:
how different are my thoughts
since last we met.
The musings of my head
have changed considerably since then.
As I look back to what I was
I see a stranger.

THE WIND MACHINE

It is a shaft stuck into the ground—
planted by the only nearby tree.
The shaft has several arms that extend
in a "praise the Lord" fashion.
On the arms are cups
designed to catch the wind
and as they do those arms twirl.
On a breezy day
their motions mesmerize an old man
who sits back comfortably
and sips a drink with a little zip.

He can sit there for a long time
and think about inconsequential things
as he watches those raised arms
go round and round and round—
sometimes watching 'til the sun goes down.

THOUGHTFUL

He is very thoughtful—
not especially considerate—
but he is full of thoughts.
They cascade into his consciousness
just behind his waking.
Some of them hold hands.
They beckon him to catch them
and often flee beyond his reach.
Others he subdues
and then embraces.
That is how his day begins
before he sets his feet upon the floor.

THE WRONG THING

Over the years
I've often heard it said
(especially at funerals)
God does not give you
more than you can bear.
I don't think so!
I've known folks
who, in my opinion
have had too much.
It doesn't seem to me
that God dispenses
either grief or pain
in measured quantities.
It's often difficult
to say the right thing
in many situations.
Offering silence is better
than the wrong thing.

THOUGHTS ABOUT THOUGHTS

I do not tell my heart to beat
nor ask my lungs to breathe.
I tell my body parts to move—
within their limits they perform.

But thoughts are quite another thing.
Sometimes I think I'm in control—
that what I think I will.
But then my mind is often lured away
by what, I cannot say.
I find I'm thinking thoughts some days
I never thought I'd think.

I think I'll be this way for quite a while
and though I wish for more control
I love to be surprised
by all the unexpected things
that come to mind.

FEELINGS

MY FOOTPRINTS

Moisture gathered in the night
was laid upon the wooden bridge
waiting for my footsteps in the dawn.

My footprints then
began to make
their mark upon that dew.

I saw them point toward me
when I returned—
that set me to wondering.

And thus I thought about
the marks that I have made—
the marks that I have made
as I've collected many years.

I wasn't especially impressed
with the history that I recollect.

But still, the opportunity TO BE
never ceases to amaze me
and I'm so pleased
I've been allowed
my simple destiny.

APPLE PIE THERAPY

As the darkness seen through windows
began to take on gray
it was the beginning of his day.
And he was found eating homemade apple pie.

He thought of the falling DOW
and the bitterness in politics
and growing old.

The pie was succulent!
Though he tried to find despair
it was not there
even when his dish was empty.

DOG

The philosopher, Nietzsche
dealt with a lot of pain
in his latter years.
He named his pain DOG.
His dog was faithful
and followed him around
all the day long.
When he went to bed at night
he was right there with him
snuggling beside him.
In the morning he was nearby
and as he went through his day
Dog was never far away.

MY CONTOUR SANDER

Some folks
have love affairs
with machines.
I'm one of those.

We fall in love
because
they serve our needs so well
and offer pleasure when employed.

My contour sander:
a turn-on for me
every time I turn it on.

Just a round, air-filled drum
wrapped with an abrasive sleeve
has shaped my life
enabling me to shape
the work I've done
for many years.

QUARTERED OAK

While prayers were being said in church
I bowed my head but didn't close my eyes.
My eyes began to wander to the pew in front of me
and there I saw the signs of quartered oak—
unique and beautiful they are.
When certain oak trees are milled in certain ways
their grain displays are so compelling
that a man at prayer
might be glad to be where
he can, with pleasure, stare
at what God and man together have designed.

IT DID NOT HAVE TO BE THIS WAY

When it all started
it could have been different—
couldn't it?
After all
God had a choice.
He was free
and He decided to put it in gear
and to go forward
where He wanted to go.
So he made us eventually
(it took long enough)
and we are told
we are made in His image.
So we choose, too,
but it didn't turn out
the way we expected—
at least, I think that's true for most of us.
I guess it's OK to wonder
if it could have been different—
your life and mine.
But there's not much
we can do about it now
and maybe we never could.

NORMAL FOLKS

Sometimes I belong here—
sometimes I don't—
that is
if belonging is a feeling—
not a fact.

Even the roads I walk upon
are foreign and familiar
depending on my state of mind.

I resist community
and cherish friendships.

How strange are my complexities!

Yet I've no monopoly
on being slightly out of step
with normal folks.

Could be:
there are no normal folks.

OLD LOVE

Love, when all its passions fade—
when it's seen embracing years
to honor and to hold and care
is worth far more than rapture.

Love maintained through joy and sorrow—
love grown stronger in the storms
that strain and stress the aging bonds
transcends all ecstasy.

Love renewed as it grows old—
which offers depths one never dreamed of
when life was in its infancy—
it blesses more than bliss.

Love which hones its coping skills
to deal with life's contingencies
when the unexpected comes
exceeds all inspiration.

We elderly so often see
long love, its final flourishing
awarding gifts of staying power
to many of those encumbered.

PAIN

I tried on pain the other day
and saw it didn't fit right
upon my aging body.
I have some friends
who wear it pretty well—
they're more tolerant than I.
I tried to smile
and made my lips curl up
but didn't feel the smile.
I turned stoic
and grit my teeth
and thought I'd not complain.
But soon my disposition
revealed my happy self
had somehow disappeared.
So I will try to wait it out
and hope that time
will bring the matter to a close.
Should it not I'll seek
some better strategies for coping.

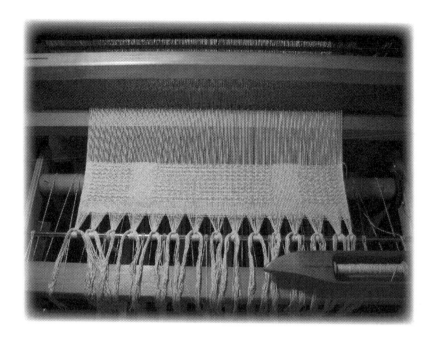

THE WEAVING

Sometimes sadness leaves
like a sunset fading in the west.
Sometimes it's more swift to exit—
like a light turned off.
Or it may fade so slowly
we'll be unaware entirely
and may even try to find it.

This is true of gladness, too.
Both of these consume
our heart's excursions
wandering around beneath our minds
and often shaping what we think.

Sadness and gladness are strands
woven into the fabric of our lives
and when we are old, if we get to be so
we can look back and see the weaving.

THE HAUNTED MEAT EATER

I like to fry bacon
and likewise like to eat it.
But I've had moments
when the spirits of pigs
have caused me to waiver.
They come to me pleading
suggesting to me that beef is better.
Cattle sometimes haunt me
and urge me to choose poultry.
Chickens encourage me to think of lamb.
I can understand their points of view
and were I on the menu
I'd be haunting, too.

THE SHORE

Out of the water
and on to land
our forebears came.
Evolution's claim we understand.

So many of us are drawn to the shore
there where primordial feelings stored
are stirred.

Now staring at the sea
the brevity of me
is touched by the eternal.

By watching waves
my smallness in the scheme of things
does not deter my wonder.

I MOURN AND CELEBRATE

I mourn and celebrate most every day—
days never so dark I cannot marvel—
never so bright that sadness does not intervene.
We're made for laughter—made for tears.
And if the years do anything at all
they deepen my conviction
that fate is very fickle.
Most people
do not earn so many of their joys
nor do they reap
the misery that befalls them.

THE PAINTED BIRD

There is a painted blue bird
that inhabits
the bottom of my cereal bowl
and it clings to a painted branch.
Each morning
I cover him up
with my choice of
Wheaties or Corn Flakes
or Rice Krispies
or various puffs.
Then I pour on milk
with a dash of cream
sprinkle on a tad of sugar
and dig away with a spoon
'til I reach that bird.
Some days I fear
that when I scoop and chew
and swallow
and come to the end
of my breakfast repast
that the little bird
will not be there
but will have flown away—
or maybe—
or maybe
I have swallowed it.

PSSSCHHH

The forecast: "Possible showers".
My forecast after checking
the morning sky: "Likely showers".

So I took an umbrella with me
on my morning walk. I enjoyed
swinging it back and forth—
left hand then right hand.
When I passed a fellow walker
he or she received a serious wave.

I thought: "If my grandson were here
he'd make a rifle from this thing
and go pssschhh! pssschhh!"
I cannot spell the sound
but I can make it and I did
while aiming here and there.

If there were those who saw me
they're likely wondering still.
My precautions proved unnecessary
but provided me with pleasure
I would have been denied
had they not been heeded.

THE NICKEL

I wasn't expecting it
and when I came near it
I was walking along
looking at the landscape
hardly aware of where my feet were taking me.
By chance, I looked down.
There, by the edge of the road
I saw it shining
though covered with a little sand.
I stopped, bent down
and picked it up: a NICKEL.
It could have been a buried treasure
for the pleasure it evoked.
I wiped it off, examined it
and put it in my pocket, feeling pleased
and wondering just a bit about its history—
'twas dated nineteen sixty.

I'm glad that I'm still capable of joy
that little things provide.
When I was young
I thought that old folks
couldn't feel as I so often did—
and still so often do.

THE SOCK MARKET

I have vicious big toe nails
and the right one
is more vicious than the left.
They eat socks—
the toes of socks
and they grieve me a little
but grieve my wife more
because she's in charge
of my socks
and buys new ones when
I need them.
I cut my toe nails
on a regular basis
so it's not my neglect
that causes this problem—
it's just the way it is
and the way it's been
since I've started keeping watch
over the fact that
I go through a lot of socks
and thus aid and abet
the sock market.

WITH SILENCE ON MY GRAVE

I gave up measuring God
some time ago—
even giving Him or Her or It a name.
(I'll use He for your convenience.)

He has grown considerably
since I used to call Him names—
or so it seems to me.
He often overwhelms me
and He rebuffs my verbal overtures.
I cannot nail Him down
though I have tried to paint him
with my practiced pen.

Once a preacher
I've given up proclaiming
or persuading
or even reading holy writ.

And when I'm gone
the folks who love me
will be apprised
that all is well with me
with silence on my grave.

NATURE

A MAP OF THE MOON

I've been moved by the moon as most of you
know—
I have seen it come and have seen it go.
I'm awed by the various shapes I've seen—
a moon when full and a moon when lean.
But I didn't learn 'til a short time ago
that some very smart men whom I don't know
made a detailed map of all the moon's places
while I made up poems of all the moon's faces.
This map was made back in two thousand nine
and I'll bet that the map contains no rhyme of
mine.
However, I can't help but be quite amazed
with what those astronomers did with their days
while I messed around with pen and ink
to suggest to friends just what I think
about our moon that swells and shrinks.

But even if some have to wax scientific
they still must acknowledge: the moon's terrific!

A VIEW FROM HERE

From my recliner
I see them scrubbing
oil soaked birds.
The birds look like:
"What the hell is going on?"
as they endure
the ministrations
that will save them.
There are still
plenty of good folk
offering various kinds of healing
to our ravaged world.
I sit here and applaud
and sometimes write a check.

BRIEF ENCOUNTER

It wasn't that the birds stopped singing
as they had been throughout my walk—
it was that a skunk appeared quite suddenly
coming out of a nearby drain pipe
and I ceased to hear their morning symphony.
He came to a stop, as did I,
examining his degree of danger, as did I.
He didn't turn his back on me—
a sure sign of skunk hostility.
Nor did I turn my back on him
for I had no weaponry back there—
at least very little.
It took a while for both of us to see
that neither of us meant to harm.
I began to hear again bird song
and then I walked along.

DAY LILIES

This time of year
when lilies bloom
they also sleep—
begin to fold their petals up
just as the sun starts sinking.

Their loveliness remains obscure
through all the hours of night.

But when the sky brings dawn
they open to the world again
and by the time that I walk by
they're half way to the beauty
that astounds the human eye.

THE STALWART DAFFODILS

When the frost lies on the daffodils
and the whims of spring are still uncertain
they bow in unison, as if in prayer—
a yellow congregation subdued but strong.
When the sun begins to touch their petals
they very slowly change their pious posture
and begin to lift their gleaming heads
to face a day that's moving toward the summer.
By the time the daffodils are gone
the frost will cease to threaten growing things
and all the fragile flowers will survive.
And winter's wrath will surely be forgotten.

LUCKY WORM

The worm had chosen incorrectly
and tried to squirm on asphalt
confusing it with soil
and not having sufficient mental prowess
to discern the difference.

Along came a man who saw its plight—
bent down and flipped that wiggly thing
with a fingertip
to a landscape more amenable.

Not only that
when the early bird came
and sought that worm for prey
the same man stood up and shooed it away
and saved that worm for another day
of dealing with its constant danger.

THE LEAVES ARE STILL

The world outside my window
is so still that it calls me to look carefully
to double check its status as motionless.
What stirs in the slightest breeze
is not stirring now.
I am the one moved by this condition.
What is there about this quietude
that engages this heart of mine?
I had no intention of becoming prayerful
but I find myself in a sacred place
where holiness has invaded my being.
I will ask for nothing and will be given
more than I deserve.

THE LEAVES BEGAN TO STIR

Leaning on the railing of the bridge
I saw the image of the live oak tree
reflected on the surface of the lake.
I took in its shape, its branches—
and focused on its leaves
so motionless—without a quiver.
And for a time their stillness entered me
and took possession of my soul.

Then suddenly the leaves began to stir
responding as the wind came up
from out of nowhere, to break the spell and to
erase the momentary beauty
in which I'd found such peace.

WAITING FOR THE STORMS

The leaves are stiller than still—
not a breath of air is moving.
There is distant thunder.
I am waiting, as are the trees.
Soon I'll hear rain drops
fall upon the deck—
about the time the wind arrives
to make so many branches dance.

I've been through this before
and surely you have, too.
How many times
in over eighty years?
I can scarce remember how it was
when I was young—
but I believe I've never been unmoved
while waiting for the storms to come.

THE FROST

On the last day of April
the last frost of spring
was laid upon
the roof tops, lawns and flowers here.
I watched the sparkling silver
slowly disappear.
Sunbeams came through trees
like giant straws—
sucked up the ice
'til there was none at all.
Some fragile flowers died.
Those that survived
were covered thoughtfully
by those forewarned
that frost was on its way.

TREE-SPEAK

As I walked by the live oak trees
'twas more than sight
that drew me there.

I could feel their presence
well beyond what I could see.

And so I stopped awhile beneath
a few—the few
which especially drew me
to be embraced by their shade.
Though I chose that closeness
I knew that I'd been chosen—
that they'd been watching me
and waiting for me as I passed by.

Surely there are other folks
who know the joy of tree-speak
but on this particular morning
and in a particular place
it was only I who heard them.

GEESE

When Canada geese
fly overhead
honking and appearing beautiful
it almost takes your breath away.

But if a few of them should land
and stay awhile
it becomes propitious for you
to watch where you are stepping.

Many things in life
look better at a distance.

IN THE SMOKIES

Between the many hills
a mist had settled—
lying in the valleys.
It snuck in furtively
about the time we came to look
and wrapped itself around those hills
so we could only see their tops.
It was as if some clouds had dropped
to claim the lower portions of the earth—
a shroud that covered all but peaks.
We watched
until the night made all that eerie beauty
disappear.

But then when morning came
the scene became reversed.
The tops of all those hills
had vanished in the clouds
and we could only see so high
and then our vision ceased.
We had to guess what lay beyond their slopes.

MORNING

IT'S FIVE A.M.

I believe it's Saturn's glow
now coming through the trees.
But I don't really know.
Perhaps it's Venus, maybe Mars—
something very far!

Inspired but not educated in celestial affairs
I look upward every night
and early in the mornings
and I am moved by what I see.
Though I have learned that planets are not stars
it doesn't matter much to me
for what I feel and see
is in the realm of inspiration—not delineation.
The heavens speak to those who comprehend
and map the space above.
But many of us quite ignorant
are moved by galaxies.
We marvel at the intricacies that lace our skies.

AS NIGHT WAS SLOWLY DISAPPEARING

I began my walk
as night was slowly disappearing.
I looked up at the center of the sky
and saw a crescent moon
dissolving its surrounding darkness.
And then the gray above me
took on hues of blue.
Some eastern clouds
in little pieces
started glowing orange
to harbinger the coming of the sun.
I didn't think that anything could tarnish
this beginning of another day.

STAR MELTING TME

It happens most mornings
early
when folks around here
are still sleeping.
It's not spectacular
like the sunrise.

Who wants to pay attention
to stars fading
when another hour in bed
is so desirable?
Probably a few fools
who don't need much
to turn them on—
like stars turning off.

So quietly does it happen—
this silent exit of their light.
I wonder if the birds
and critters in the woods
take notice.

THE CLOUDS AS ACTORS

As dawn creeps into day
the eastern clouds pretend
that they're a mountain range
just above the tops of trees.

Then they pretend
that they've been finger painted
by little ones who think
the sky's an easel:
blue and red—orange and green.
My—what a scene!

And then they fall apart
and start to climb the canopy
beneath which they employ
their magic right before my eyes.

And then they're white
and take the shapes of animals
which parade across the sky.

Their stage is easily accessed.
Their shows are different every day
and no one has to pay.

THE GIANT BROOM

The early sun
makes long tree shadows
that sweep across the frost
that lies upon the lawn.

I see the shadows
as a giant broom
that sweeps away
the silver from the grass.

And though I know
the frost would melt
without the work of shadows
my mind would rather
play with possibilities
kindled by imagination
than know the scientific reason
for the frost's demise.

THE MAGIC MOMENT

I like to be there
when
there isn't any light—
and then—
and then there is.
I like to see the day sneak over trees
and onto roof tops
as it begins
to turn the darkened sky to morning.
It may not matter to the day
that I am there—
I'm sure it doesn't care.
But I do.

THE SKY IS MUTE

The sky is mute this morning—
has nothing to say—
not even a suggestion
of possibilities.
It wears a veil
to hide its beauty
and I can only guess
what it is holding back.

THE SKY COMES DOWN AT DAWN

The pond is glass this morning
taking the dawn sky
and laying it beneath me
so I can see its upside-downess
just beyond my toes.
A little circle resembling
a dropped pebble's wake
intrudes this celestial reflection—
and then another—and another.
Some little fish, oblivious to my scene
start their routines
but make waves of such little stature
they hardly interrupt the smoothness
that makes the sky come down.

THE SUN NO LONGER RISES WHERE IT DID

The sun no longer rises where it did—
for I'm hundreds of miles away
from where I used to be
when I saw the light come through the trees
early in the morning.
And that makes a world of difference
where the sun comes up for me.
It will take some getting used to
but the sun will find me willing
to change what I can see
early in the morning.

EVENING

A STRANGE FOCUS

Though I try to trace my journey into sleep—
to watch the path that leads me into dreams
where every night I wander, I cannot keep
my vigilance alert enough, it seems.

I clear my mind of every cluttered thought
and focus only on the coming nothingness
before arriving there. It seems I ought
to grasp the threshold. I fail I must confess.

This is a strange and esoteric task
amidst a world so fraught with pain and sorrow.
Surely there are other things to ask.
My mind could be assessed as being narrow.

Yet tonight again I'll try to see
what has heretofore avoided me.

A WINTER SOLSTICE SONNET

When it seems the darkness comes too soon
and it feels the journey of the sun too swift
to dissipate the shadows and the gloom
that sometimes claim my world, I'd gladly shift
this plight if I could only make a wish
and change the ways our days come to an end—
their bleakness now so undiminished.
But on the winter solstice we depend.
No amount of praying will affect
the way our spinning earth tilts toward the sun.
We do not suffer from divine neglect
and must admit that's not the way it's done.
Be hopeful when you look into the sky
but save your prayers for when you look inside.

BEAUTY'S DEMANDS

Notice all the people rushing by
with little time to look up at the sky.
The setting sun is frequently ignored
by passersby who think they can afford
to wait—to see it at a later date—
a more convenient time. Perhaps too late
they might decide to see the sun go down
and learn there's little beauty to be found.
Those who hesitate, then only offer
glances—
those who demure when beauty first advances
may miss its overtures. One must invest
offering attention. For beauty's best
is given to those willing to be still—
who stop, pause, and look up to the hills.

DREAMS OF MINE

Most dreams of mine
I cannot find
when wakefulness appears.
I see them slowly fade away
becoming strangers
when just a while ago
they held me in their charms.
But every now and then
a dream replays itself
and then replays itself again.
These dreams I remember
and carry them around with me—
consulting them from time to time
and wondering why they're mine.
I consider the connections
between the world I know
and one I've spawned in sleep
and find mysterious.

I HOPED TOO SOON

It seemed when I first went out to see the moon
that its path to the west was clear. I saw no clouds
as it climbed the eastern sky. I hoped too soon.
The clarity dissolved so swiftly, for a distant shroud
as if on a mission to obstruct the lunar light
began its task. At first some stars disappeared
that lay in its path. But the moon became out of sight
almost before I could grasp it. The eclipse seemed weird.
The darkness that came seemed to be a hovering darkness—
it had a presence that I began to feel.
It was so strange—this evening's sudden starkness.
No other way to say it—it was surreal.
Since then I hesitate when I see a sky
without a cloud at night—and I know why.

ONE PARTICULAR FULL MOON

The small pond in the valley
whose surface was like glass
because of the windless night
did not reflect the full moon
'til it was almost midnight.

And when it did
the reflection resembled
an egg in a frying pan
sunny side up.

Soon the egg slid off center
and eventually spilled
into the grassy shore
and was absorbed—
but some star specks remained
floating around.

SLEEP

The night descends and carries me away.
The darkness comes extinguishing the day
and then the pillow on my bed conforms
to certain contours of my head. I leave
the world behind and join another place
so different from a usual day's unfolding.
How it is with you I do not know
but surely off to slumber land you go.

We may or may not dream in this departure.
We may resist its entree, or we may
yield, a respite from quotidian demands.
But we share it with the human race.
The harbors of our sleeping vary widely—
for some it's mansions—others, beneath a bridge.
But all of us must yield—must give ourselves
to darkness, fleeing what we've made of time
and often finding peace and restoration.

SLIPPERY DREAMS

Most of my dreams
are slippery ones
evading all my efforts
to reel them in
early in the morning.

My mind goes fishing
in the night
and often finds
such strangeness there.

What I pull forth
doesn't seem to live much
beyond my awakening eyes.

Though now and then
I catch and hold one
that can't elude
the grasp of memory.

SOME DAYS END

Some days end
and you wish they'd last forever.
Some days end
and you can't wait for them to cease.

Some days end
and you know you'll remember them.
Some days end
and it seems that nothing has occurred.

Some days end
and you wonder where the time has gone.
Some days end
when you thought the clocks had stopped.

Some days end
and you've been saddened by some tragic news
and some days end
and you've been surprised by joy.

Some days end
and your faith feels so strong.
Some days end
and you can't believe in anything.

Some days end
and you write a poem or two.
Some days end
and your ink runs dry.

THE EVENING OF THE 4TH

On the evening of the 4th of July
I expect to sit in an Adirondack chair
and watch fireflies punctuate
the emerging darkness.
I'll listen to a symphony by cicadas.
As the dusk begins to deepen
I'll look above and see the stars.
I'll not go far for this enjoyment
and when it's done
they'll not be many steps to take
until I'll find my place and go to sleep.

THE JOYS OF TWILIGHT

After the sun had fled the western sky—
before the night had come
to claim the trees that offered my horizon
I sat in an Adirondack chair
and found a mood akin to prayer.
The birds had stopped their songs
but crickets stole the silence.
I had hoped to find a poem somewhere
by sitting there and waiting for the muse.
I felt the darkness come
and slowly cover me with stars.
The speeches from the earth and sky
I heard and now attempt to share.
So join me in the joys of twilight.

THE SHAPE OF THE MOON

The moon becomes misshapen
as its fullness disappears
to watchers of the night
who note its shrinking shape
as time goes by.

Those drawn to its roundness
become less interested
when the lunar sphere
begins to take on shadows.

It shrinks a little every day and night
until its visual status
becomes appealing as a crescent.

Even as a sliver in the sky
it draws so many eyes.

But then it vanishes awhile
and stars that never go away
receive celestial adoration.

But when the lunar light begins again
the stars leave center stage
as the moon becomes the star
for many of us scanners
of our canopy above the earth.

TWILIGHT TIME

At first we saw
small patches of the sunlight
shine upon the pasture.
And they slowly moved
toward distant trees
which they climbed with ease
to reach their very top.
And then it was the clouds
that took the orange rays
and turned them pink.
We stayed
until the sky turned gray
and began
to welcome stars.

WHEN EVENINGS COME

Some days, when their evenings come
I can't wait to nestle in my bed.
The day's been heavy
and its close can't come too soon.

Some days, when their evenings come
I marvel at the speed of time
and think I need another hour or two
before I heed the call to sleep.

But I have noticed as my years progress
I'm less and less inclined
to want my nights to stretch
to witness Cinderella's flight.

MEMORY / MEMORIES

A MEMORY KINDLED

In the crowded store
near CHECKOUT
the little girl—
not real little (six-ish)
waved at me—
a sort of shy wave
so as to be unnoticed
except by me.
I did not recognize her
at first
and then became aware
that I had read stories
and poems
to her first grade class
late last spring.
Then my
questionable smile
became broad
and met head on
with hers.
Soon thereafter
she followed her mother
out of the store—
each one of us
with a good memory
kindled.

AGAINST ALL ODDS

Eighty Christmases ago, plus one
between the WAR TO END ALL WARS
and World War II, my life had just begun.
Now my waning memory has stored
a few more wars, plus many killing fields
around the globe. And here I sit, secure
wondering what this century will yield
even as my recollections blur.

The clashes of the darkness and the light
I've seen—have been involved in some—
have been amazed to see the bleakest nights
turn toward the dawn—some battles finally won.

And now we're poised to celebrate new birth.
Against all odds we pray for peace on earth.

ANOTHER LIVES WITHIN ME

I can't control my memory.
You can't control yours either!
'Tis as if ANOTHER lives within me
visiting me with thoughts and scenes.
And some of them I'd rather not recall.
Each day we meet within my head
conversing in our silent way.
My memory has its say
and only quiets with distractions
or when I'm deeply into NOW.
Before I go to sleep at night
my memory often plays with me—
although I leave it be
when I am planning for tomorrow.

A STRANGE BLESSING

In these days
when memory is apt to slip a bit
and forgetting seems to be quite frequent
perhaps you can apply that loss to your advantage
and forget the things you'd rather not recall.

If you can remember to forget these things
you'll be happier than you were before you didn't.

HARVESTING A MEMORY

Last night
a dream I had
harvested a memory.

That's often the case.

I was sailing on a small lake
in my small sailboat
with a friend I'd not seen
in more than forty years.

It was indeed a pleasure
to be with him again
on forgotten waters.

I could not have crafted
a happier dream than this
and I certainly appreciate
whatever is within me
that did.

I AM LIKE A STONE

When I am no longer
I will be a memory slowly fading—
a memory slowly fading—
slowly fading—
fading.
I am like a stone
dropping in smooth water.
The water ripples in ever-increasing circles—
circles whose height diminishes
with each expanding wave.
Later, the stillness forgets the stone.
There will come a time
when no one will remember.

MY FATHER INTRUDED

My father was meticulous
when hanging artificial ice cycles
on our Christmas trees.
One at a time he hung them.

His way of doing this
on a particular day
intruded on my morning walk
as I took in the way the Spanish moss
was hanging from the live oak trees.

My father would approve.

His way of hanging things on trees
would coincide with nature's way—
a thought I never entertained
'til suddenly it came to me
while on an ordinary walk
amongst the beauty
I sometimes take for granted.

NEARLY FORTY YEARS AGO

Some twenty miles to the south
over the waters I now gaze upon
is a beach I once sailed to
from this very shore
nearly forty years ago
in a ten foot ten inch boat that I had built—
great therapy for a midlife crisis.

It is morning now, and calm
and sea gulls wait for the day on rocks
with different memories than mine
and with different hopes
for their unfolding hours.

Now I see two men in a red row boat
the same color as the sails
that once powered me over the Sound.
They are gliding over its surface
heading toward the red of the rising sun.
Perhaps they, too, will have this day to recall
when their years assemble
and have forged fond memories.

NOSTALGIA

I go back, sometimes
when time's demands are few
to locate some sadness or some joy
that I have visited before.

I do not want the past
to vanish from my memory
lest I lose what I embraced—
what I loved
and have not ceased to love
in spite of endings.
I must be careful
not to stay too long
but revisiting what was
is part of what it is to be.

STORAGE

I don't know where the forgotten go
when they've left my mind.
When it seems they've gone forever
they sometimes strangely reappear
triggered by some occasion
or some sight or sound.
Then I remember—
remember that I'd forgotten
and then I begin to wonder
whatever happened to them.

Soon I'll forget this poem I write.
I expect that you will, too.
Likely it will vanish forever
and go where all things go
that aren't retained.

TYING SHOES

Sometimes
when I tie my shoes
I think of when
I first learned to tie them
which was quite a while ago.
And I recall
the struggle that it was
to get it right—
how proud I felt
when I could do it by myself.

For many years
I hadn't thought of how it was back then.
But now
that reaching down to tie my shoes
is not as easy as it was
I think of when
it wasn't easy at the start.

LOSS

AND ISN'T ANYMORE

I can't quite
accept the fact
that he was
and isn't any more
nor can I grasp
how those
who've loved so well
can deal with losses
greater than mine—
who seem able to accept
better than I
what has been taken from them.
That the Lord gives
and takes away
may be how it is
but I abhor it
and rile against it.
Anger sometimes
drives my grief
and saps my gratitude
for what was
and isn't anymore.

COPING

When those we love
are carried away in the arms of death
and leave us only carrying memories
we may try to wear the mantle of gratitude
but we often weep.

No matter how colorful
we paint the lives
of those beyond the grave
they're times when grieving pains
make claims upon our dailyness.

We sometimes fight the fading of our recollections
for we wish to savor what we've cherished.

JENNIFER DIED

When Jennifer O'Dench died
she was eleven—
a schoolmate of my daughter.

There was so little I could say
to touch her world of sadness.

I used to think
that growing up
meant understanding mysteries—
that there were always explanations—
that one could offer more than consolation.

But I got old enough
to feel a mighty helplessness
when standing by a grave.

I'D HANDLE IT A DIFFERENT WAY

What can we rage against—
we who've come to be
so filled with years—
surviving still amidst a world
where rage is coming to be common?

Perhaps because of how it's been for us
we can only manage to be distraught
that time has brought us to a place
where losing seems to be a way of life.
Not many days go by
when news of someone
somewhat near to us
has disappeared in death—
or even worse, someone we love.
Not only do connections shrink—
our bodies send us messages
we'd rather not take notice of
but unsuccessfully ignore.

There are some folks I know
who take it all in stride
and seem to thrive in spite of losses.
But I am disappointed
in God's methodology of closure.
Were I in charge
I'd handle it a different way.

I FEEL THEM GOING DOWN

When the rain subsided
the landscape glistened.
The sun above the western trees glowed red.
Then as it set the sky turned pink.
Its colors slowly faded
and then vanished.

Sadness suddenly surrounded me
and melancholy crept in with the shadows.
Too many folks I know
now emulate the earth at sunset.
Sometimes I feel them going down.

INDEX

D

E

G

H

I

V

W

PHOTO CREDITS

Front cover photo by Thomas Fay Vary.
All other photos by Joanne Vary Schwandes.
In order of appearance:

1. [Front Cover] Silver Maple. 4 Feb 2012. Along the St. Lawrence River, Cape Vincent NY.
2. [Relationships] Sandhill Crane Family. 18 Feb 2007. Good Samaritan Society—Kissimmee Village, Kissimmee FL.
3. [Transitions] Cypress Knees. 28 Jan 2012. Osceola County Schools Reedy Creek Environmental Center, Kissimmee FL.
4. [GOD'S FINGER] God's Finger. 14 Aug 2007. On a tombstone in an old cemetery, Jefferson County NY.
5. [HOUSED IN A TORTOISE SHELL] Galapagos Tortoise. 10 Mar 2010. Isabela Island, Galapagos, Ecuador.
6. [Reflections] Tree Reflection. 27 Mar 2009. Shingle Creek, Kissimmee FL.
7. [THE WIND MACHINE] Russ's Wind Machine. 7 Apr 2012. Good Samaritan Society—Kissimmee Village, Kissimmee FL.

8. [Feelings] Sea Lions at Rest. 11 Mar 2010. Isabela Island, Galapagos, Ecuador.

9. [MY CONTOUR SANDER] Russ and His Contour Sander. 7 Aug 2012. Woodworking Shop, Good Samaritan Society—Kissimmee Village, Kissimmee FL.

10. [THE WEAVING] Weaving a Bamboo Shawl. 19 Nov 2009. Good Samaritan Society—Kissimmee Village, Kissimmee FL.

11. [THE SHORE] Shore. 7 May 2007. St. Augustine Beach, St. Augustine FL

12. [Nature] Full Moon. 12 May 2008. Sunset Ranch Trail, Lake Marian, Kenansville FL.

13. [THE LEAVES ARE STILL] Swamp Maple Leaves. 2 Apr 2011. Osceola County Schools Reedy Creek Environmental Center, Kissimmee FL.

14. [TREE-SPEAK] Live Oak Canopy. 10 May 2009. Forever Florida, St. Cloud FL.

15. [DAFFODILS] Daffodils. 11 Mar 2012. Silver Spring MD.

16. [Morning] Spider Web with Dew. 3 Dec 2006. Merritt Island National Wildlife Refuge, Merritt Island FL.

17. [THE SKY COMES DOWN AT DAWN] Reflection on Lake Sunset. 26 May 2009. Good Samaritan Society—Kissimmee Village, Kissimmee FL.

18. [Evening] Sunset over Lake Dixie. 3 Jan 2010. Lake Louisa State Park, Clermont FL.

19. [Memory / Memories] Grandma's Hand. 20 Feb 2010. Good Samaritan Society—Kissimmee Village, Kissimmee FL.
20. [Loss] Weeping Willow. 21 Aug 2011. On a tombstone in an old cemetery, Jefferson County NY.
21. [I FEEL THEM GOING DOWN] Evening over Lake Dixie. 3 Jan 2010. Lake Louisa State Park, Clermont FL.
22. [Back Insert] Russ on his Tricycle. 22 May 2012. Good Samaritan Society—Kissimmee Village, Kissimmee FL.

Russ Peery, Age 85
On His New Tricycle